THE POWER TO CONQUER FEAR

THE POWER TO CONQUER FEAR

"FOR GOD HAS NOT GIVEN US A SPIRIT OF FEAR, BUT OF POWER AND OF LOVE AND OF A SOUND MIND"

II TIMOTHY 1:7 NKJV

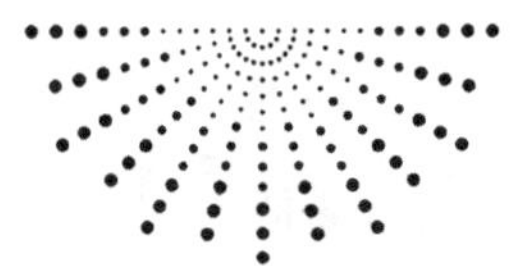

DORETHA SMITH

CONTENTS

ACKNOWLEDGMENTS

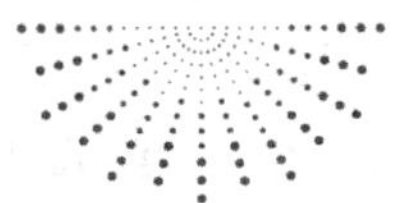

Dear Almighty God,

I am grateful for all the blessings you have bestowed upon me. I am genuinely thankful for my precious family's love, support, and encouragement.

I thank you, Lord, for my wonderful son Ellis and daughter-in-love Michelle's uplifting words, which have motivated me not to give up on writing this book. A special thanks to my granddaughter-in-love, Ashley, who has been instrumental in helping me achieve my goals. Her expertise, valuable insights, and selfless dedication have been pivotal in helping me edit my manuscript. Her support has been invaluable in making this project a success. I feel blessed to have such a wonderful family who always stands by me.

I am deeply grateful for the unwavering support and confidence of my spiritual leaders, Pastor Bishop Herman and First Lady Dr. Martha L. Crockett. Their steadfast commitment to helping me grow spiritually has been exceptional. Their guidance and mentorship have been instrumental in shaping me into the person I am today. I cannot thank them enough for their impact on my life. I want to give special thanks to First Lady Martha for taking the time to read my manuscript a few days before I decided to submit it to a publisher.

I am also thankful for the church family of Faith And Hope Temple COGIC, where I have found a spiritual home and a community that supports me in my faith journey.

I want to thank my cousins, Barbara and Earl King, for their valuable insight, encouragement, and support, as well as my excellent prayer partner, Carolyn Davis.

I also want to thank Dr. Coletta Johnson-Bey, Jennifer Taylor Monteagudo Mora, and Lora Jarrett for their invaluable feedback and words of encouragement. Your advice was constructive, helping me reset my approach and reach my target audience. I am eternally grateful to each of you and feel blessed to have you in my life.

Last but not least, I thank everyone. Even though you may not have directly played a part in reading my manuscript, you wished me well and encouraged me, and I cherish every one of you. I am grateful to God to have you.

Thank you all for your love and support.

With gratitude,

Doretha Smith

THANK YOU, LORD, FOR YOUR
AMAZING POWER!

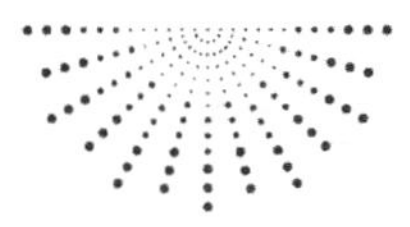

INTRODUCTION

"FOR GOD HAS NOT GIVEN US A SPIRIT OF FEAR, BUT OF POWER AND OF LOVE AND OF A SOUND MIND."

(II Timothy 1:7 NKJV)

Imagine being held captive by the spirit of fear, unable to break free from its shackles. However, if we choose to use it as a source of motivation, it can propel us forward towards success and growth.

A spirit of fear can cause us to feel anxious, worried, and scared. It can lead to avoidance of certain situations or activities and impact decision-making and overall well-being. Fear can be a paralyzing force that hinders us from achieving our goals and reaching our full potential.

The spirit of fear can also hinder us from fulfilling God's purpose in other ways. It can prevent us from taking necessary risks, trying new things, or stepping out of our comfort zone. Fear can also lead to indecision, self-doubt, and a lack of confidence, hindering our ability to pursue our calling and live according to God's purpose. Fear was my reality for years; I have experienced all these things in my life's journey.

The constant replay of negative thoughts made it difficult to focus on the present moment and move out of my comfort zone. I kept talking to God about my insecurities, fixated on my past failures, and not surrendering them to Him, who could free me. Although I have always believed in God, He has brought me through many trials and tribulations. The internal conflict between my spirit and flesh was a fierce battle. Despite the intense struggle, I often experienced the comforting presence of God - a reassuring and gentle touch. His presence served as a source of great comfort and joy. The words of (II Timothy 1:7) stirred something deep within me, becoming my solace and motivation. They encouraged me to confront my fears and embrace a life brimming with hope, love, and optimism.

My journey extends beyond personal growth; it includes the influence I can have on others, the lives I can impact, and the positive changes I can bring to the world. It bears witness to the transformative power of divine love and the hope it gives to those seeking it. With divine guidance, you can overcome your fears and live a purposeful and meaningful life.

The quote, "Don't let fear control you. Instead, use it as a source of motivation," is a powerful reminder that we should not let fear hold us back from achieving our goals. This quote is more relevant than ever in today's world, where uncertainty and challenges are the norm. It is important to acknowledge our fears and use them as a motivation to move forward and grow.

I am incredibly grateful for God's grace and a renewed mindset; through prayer and meditation on His Word, I found the strength to break free from the hold of negative fear thoughts weighing me down.

An unknown author once said, "Fear has two meanings - forget everything and run or face everything and rise. The choice is yours." And I am here to tell you that you have the power to rise above your fears and achieve greatness.

I am humbled to share my story and lessons with you at age 78. "It is evidence that breaking free from fear and living the life you've always dreamed of is always possible, no matter how late it may seem." And I pray that whoever reads these pages will find solace in my words and be inspired to triumph over any obstacles you face. With God's help, anything is possible!

1
STIRRED UP

I was stirred up! It was an unforgettable Tuesday night of April 7, 2020, marking my debut in leading a Bible lesson through Zoom, a modern platform for virtual gatherings. As the world grappled with the onset of the COVID-19 pandemic, this experience became a defining moment that has left an indelible mark on my life. Sitting in front of my computer, I felt a rush of nerves and fear, yearning for the reassuring presence of God.

In the grip of my nervousness, everything around me blurred, making it hard to concentrate. A deep sense of loneliness settled over me, aching for a connection that seemed out of reach. My mind struggled to escape the overwhelming emotions, leaving me strangely detached from reality.

I vividly remember feeling so overwhelmed that I wished I could have disappeared to escape the agony, embarrassment, and shame. I told my Pastor that I felt like everyone was staring at me.

This encounter with fear ignited a steadfast resolve in me. It has inspired me to take charge of my thoughts and transform a terrifying experience into personal growth and empowerment. What initially appeared to be a negative situation has positively impacted me.

I've heard stories of people dealing with pain by turning to alcohol, drugs, or other temporary distractions, but I'm grateful that I didn't go down that path, and I thank God for guiding me in the right direction.

On Wednesday, April 8, 2020, I took to Facebook to share my experience with fear. I boldly declared, **"Fear, you will not stop me from moving forward."** Perseverance is one of my greatest strengths, and I am determined not to give up in the face of obstacles. I've heard that the remedy for fear is to confront it. Even when I didn't feel like God was with me, I acted on what I feared. I held onto the scripture (II Timothy 1:7) as a source of strength. It feels like the start of a new chapter in my life, as I am embracing growth and learning to take my stand on scripture in my later years.

I have watched my first Facebook video and saw a scary version of myself, but I still regularly post videos on Facebook, mostly on Fridays. I decided that fear wouldn't control me anymore. I've resolved to be confident and brave! Even though I make mistakes, I'm not discouraged. I'm determined to continue speaking because I've learned from experience that the more effort you put into something, the more you improve.

I used to be held back by fear, but now I see it as a pathway to experiencing incredible things. Instead of focusing on my limitations and failures, I trust God's guidance and love. While being cautious and aware of potential dangers in certain situations is essential, the "Fear of God" is more about trust and liberation. It involves studying and meditating on God's Word, establishing a prayer life, seeking intimacy with God, and being part of a supportive community of believers. Additionally, it means obeying God's commands, aligning our lives with His will, approaching God with humility and awe, and acknowledging His sovereignty and greatness. In times of vulnerability, we must lean on our faith in God and not become consumed by our imperfections. Trusting in God's plan and seeking His strength can provide comfort and guidance during challenging times. Instead of fixating on our shortcomings, we can remind ourselves of God's love and forgiveness, allowing us to move forward with hope and renewed determination. This perspective helps us to navigate vulnerability with grace and resilience, knowing that a higher power supports us.

I have read about individuals in biblical history, which shows me that they also had human weaknesses. One notable example is Moses, who made excuses to God, expressing his feelings of inadequacy when God commissioned him to lead His people out of Egypt. Despite Moses's excuses, God assured him that He would be with him to accomplish the mission. Just as God provided for Moses when leading the people out of Egypt, He will also equip us with what we need to complete our tasks.

Apostle Peter's experience on the stormy waters of the Sea of Galilee serves as a powerful demonstration of fear and redemption. As Peter shifted his focus from God to the raging storm, fear overcame him, leading him to cry out to Jesus for salvation. This episode displays God's ability to rescue and bring calm to turbulent situations.

In challenging times, the Word of God provides steadfast comfort. Isaiah 41:10 is a profoundly comforting verse that is a powerful reminder for believers to lean on God's presence and draw strength from Him. The verse reminds us not to be afraid because God is always with us. It reassures us that God will strengthen us and help us overcome challenges. The imagery of being upheld by God's righteous right hand conveys a sense of protection and support. Overall, this verse is a powerful reminder of God's faithfulness and the source of strength and courage for those who trust Him.

Whoa! God got my attention! I had a moment on that Tuesday night of April 7, 2020, that made me realize that I had become too comfortable in my ways. My life was blessed with abundance, good health, and fulfillment, *yet I feel called by God to strive for even more*. I thank God for His longsuffering with me. He did not allow me to keep being constrained to my past experiences. Despite being in my seventies, I feel a strong sense of empowerment and freedom to pursue my purpose. I wholeheartedly believe in the divine Spirit of God's Power within me, and I am confident that I can accomplish extraordinary feats.

The early years of my past were a challenge. Life was difficult for me as a young girl who grew up on a farm in Emporia, Virginia. I was pregnant at the age of seventeen and had to drop out of school, which was a turning point in my life. It was not easy, and many difficulties came with it, making it a roller coaster ride that changed the course of my life's journey. Back then, if you did not finish high school, people treated you negatively, which caused me much pain and struggle. It was challenging to deal with the stigma, and I felt ashamed and afraid for many years.

My upbringing was in church; however, I was drawn to worldly pursuits that satisfied my desires. My mother's stern words, *"You, make your bed hard; you will lay in it,"* were a constant reminder of the consequences of my actions. I experienced some tough times as a result of my choices, and my bed truly became hard to bear.

Despite facing challenging circumstances, I persevered with determination and did not give up. Although I was hurting inwardly, I refused to let it defeat me and kept moving forward. Eventually, I was blessed with a job at the United States Postal Service. This experience taught me the importance of perseverance and determination to keep striving even going through the difficulties of life. I did not talk to anyone about my inner pain. It was a time of my past that I tried to block from my memory.

I pressed my way; I enrolled in night school. I continued to educate myself even though I felt ashamed that I did not graduate when I should have. Through it all, I finished by attending night school. I went to secretary school and learned how to type because I wanted to work my way from the basement of the Postal Service to the top of the personnel office, **and I did**!

I continued my education, enrolled in college, and majored in business administration, but I still harbored some misgivings and doubts about my life. I felt inferior and needed to be more eloquent in my speech. I took several courses in public speaking and trained with Toastmasters (a nonprofit organization that helps with general speaking skills) back in the day. One of my desires was to be a motivational public speaker traveling worldwide, but things turned out differently.

I worked extremely hard to educate myself. My sources of encouragement also were reading self-help books, meditating, doing yoga, and spending time alone. I worked with quiet determination and diligence to build my confidence. **I felt an immense sense of gratitude towards God, and I walked with unshakeable confidence in His power. Although some may have misunderstood my confidence as arrogance, and some say they saw me as sophisticated, they were unaware of the challenges I had conquered and the story behind my journey.** Despite moments when the burden of my past weighed heavily on me, I was determined not to let it hinder my progress. **A relentless drive resides within me, continually propelling me forward.**

While on this life's journey, I developed self-knowledge and some achievements, for which I am grateful. I received an associate degree from Saint Leo College, a Bachelor of Christian Education, and a master's in biblical studies from non-traditional schools. I retired from the United States Postal Service with thirty-two years of excellent service and am now my church's business administrator. I am involved with ministry and have the opportunity for continued education. **I am a woman of confidence who was ashamed of her past,**

but now I can shout and tell others that you do not have to let your past define who you are.

Oh! I will not forget where I came from - it could have been another way-*down* and *out-crying the blues*. God has always been divinely ordering my steps, even though I was caught up in worldly situations. I am now reborn to a greater consciousness of who I am and the mighty power within me. I see myself ever-expanding as God's child with power, love, and self-control. **I say confidently that you can rise above your circumstances and become the best version of yourselves. I will keep shining my light and showing and telling others what is possible!**

I make a conscious decision to refocus my mind whenever negative thoughts arise. I surrender every thought to God and claim His promises so that doubt and anxious thoughts no longer control me. I am determined to trust God and allow Him to guide my steps. The past no longer holds me captive, as I rely on the power within me to demolish every negative thought and make it obedient to God's Word. I walk in the power of God's healing and feel awakened to the tremendous power that resides within me. I am continuously building my faith and strength in the power within me to progress upward and benefit myself and others. **It does not mean I am a superwoman who never makes a mistake, always gets it right, and is always on top of the world every day.**

It takes persistent and intentional effort, but I am confident that God has taken away my fear and mourning about the past so that I can sing and tell of His glory. **He has made a way, and I shall not be afraid**. As the Psalmist rejoiced in Psalm 30:11-12, I, too, celebrate God's deliverance and declare that He has turned my mourning into joyful dancing. You have taken away my mourning clothes and clothed me with joy; I might sing praises to you and not be silent. O LORD my God, I will give you thanks forever!

Prayer of Praise!

I praise you, Lord; you know my Name; you knew me in my mother's wound before my birth. So marvelously made! Oh, God! Your Holy Spirit within me can heal everything as I allow the condition for healing to manifest. So, I speak to every organ, every fear, and every function of my body. I am whole. I no longer focus on my limitations, obstacles, failures, or fears. I count my blessings. Lord, as I go through my day, I am grateful for everything you provide for my life. I am grateful. How infinite, divine, and perfect is your Spirit that dwells in me? It governs my every step. It lifts me. It transmutes anything within me that would hinder or block me. You are God who can do exceedingly abundantly above all that I can ask or think, according to the power that works in me. All glory to you! Hallelujah! God, I praise you for your faithfulness, grace, and mercy. Praise You for all your promises in your Word.

Lord, I remember how patient and loving you have been to me. I think and meditate on your goodness. You are my inspiration! You alone are the LORD! You give life to everything. Praise your Holy Name! Amen.

2
FROM FEAR TO COURAGE

As I repeat, I am free from the grip of fear that once held me captive. This newfound courage fills me with joy and inspires me to live fully with confidence and freedom from fear. Determination, courage, and resilience have brought me to this point of a newfound liberation. I have the power of courage, and I realized that courage is not the absence of fear but the willingness to face it head-on. **The source of my courage is my faith in God, which moved me to meditate on II Timothy 1:7; therefore, I held onto the promise that God had given me power, love, and a sound mind rather than a spirit of fear.** I have learned that the more I exercised my courage, the stronger I became.

I am grateful for the divine push from Almighty God that gave me the power of courage to overcome the fear of my past, which once seemed impossible. It has opened up new opportunities that I never thought possible. By relying on my faith and cultivating courage, I have faced challenges that I may not have been able to face before, helping me become mentally and emotionally more assured.

Therefore, I know and believe that as long as I continue to rely on my faith in God, I will always have the courage to face whatever comes my way. It has given me the confidence to step out of my comfort zone without feeling shame, which has led to my spiritual, personal, and professional development.

I am glad I could eventually share my story with my *wonderful dear son, Ellis, who* lived with my mother until age ten and came to live with me at eleven. I have had moments where I wished I had done things differently. In hindsight, *what is important is that we learn from those moments and strive to be better moving forward.* I now have the courage to talk freely, boldly, and fearlessly about my past without being afraid.

For many years, I avoided conversations about my past, not just with my son but with others as well. **While on this journey, there was a season in my life that could have been my demise or long years in jail. When others have ill-treated you, your nature tends to want to strike back. I was lost, hurt, and broken still in the world, pleasing my flesh.**

But, in solitude and silence, I heard the voice of God - you have a son to raise. It was like a light that came into my head. I knew it was time for me to pull back from the world and focus on raising my son and getting him through school.

Praise God he graduated from high school, enrolled in college, and continued with his life. He later married a beautiful lady who was not only beautiful on the outside but also had a beautiful heart. In conversation with her, my lovely daughter-in-love, Michelle, I also shared my past with her. She said, "Mom, you can write a book." *Uhm, I thought not me.*

Also, I had never imagined that I would find the courage and strength to open up about my past pain during a phone call with my pastor and first lady one night. During our conversation, she told me that I could write a book. My spiritual leaders, Bishop Herman and First Lady Dr. Martha Crockett, are extraordinary people—so loving and down-to-earth! No matter what my situation is, they are a reliable source of encouragement to me.

My First Lady is the author of several books, and she cited her experiences with pain in her writing "The Power of Forgiveness," mainly in Chapter 3, page 35, where she stated, "Inner Pain Will Make You Bitter or Better." She states that it may not always be clear what role inner pain plays in accomplishing what God has already intended for us, but one thing is clear: inner pain will make us bitter or better. Our experiences may be instrumental in fulfilling God's purpose and plan in our lives. When it comes to internal pain, there is no exception. She recalls the enemy's work earlier in the ministry of her and her husband.

The First Lady states I will forever believe this heart-throbbing experience came to build my spiritual tenacity; it also revealed my character. While I experienced pain and anger, somewhere during my struggle, I realized that the trial made me better instead of bitter. I became more equipped to love people despite their hurting me. In Chapter IV, Dr. Crockett gives us the remedy for Inner Healing. **"FORGIVE,"** "If you are bitter, forgive and let the hurt begin to heal."

When my First Lady said I could author my book, I said I did not know about a book. I thought no one would be interested in reading about my life. I am not a known person. However, this was negative and unhealthy thinking. I have read other peoples' books born out of their experiences. Therefore, I now know from my experiences that God will use your trials, troubles, temptations, and people in your life to bring out the good. Thanks to my loving daughter-in-love, Michelle, and my loving First Lady, who saw in me what I did not see in myself.

3

DIVINE INSPIRATION MOVED ME TO BEGIN WRITING

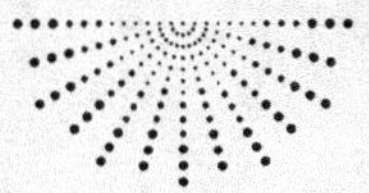

It's amazing how God's power can inspire us to act and fulfill our purpose. Deciding to start writing at the age of 75 is a testament to the extraordinary power of God! The human mind's capacity to remain sharp and competent even as it ages is remarkable. I'm inspired by the idea that I can still exercise my mental faculties to document my life story at seventy-plus. It's a testament to the resilience and enduring potential of the human spirit.

I was excited but also had mixed feelings about the thought of authoring a book; nevertheless, I set a goal to finish writing by the end of March 2021. However, I was slowing down writing while telling myself, "Doretha, you will finish," but procrastination had stepped in, and I had stopped writing for a long time, but I slowly started writing on my manuscript again even though I was starting to lose my enthusiasm at this late stage. I have been contemplating everything concerning my life and kept procrastinating. I am not interested in traveling around the world now, so I asked myself why I should continue writing. At this point, why not just give copies of my manuscript to my family? But I kept feeling a nudge in my spirit not to give up. Thanks to God's unique plan for our life.

Wow! The power, wisdom, and knowledge of God are beyond our human understanding. It is amazing to think that we cannot even begin to fathom His decisions and methods. He is great and sovereign over all things. It is humbling to realize that His thoughts are infinitely higher than ours. As the Bible says, "For my thoughts are not your thoughts, neither are your ways my ways, saith the Lord."

While I was not consciously focused on the Power within me, I now know God was guiding my steps. God always has our best interests at heart. He puts people in our path to help us. I thank God for the two dear and beautiful ladies, ministers of God, whom I spoke of earlier and who inspired me to author my story. They initially sowed the seed and watered it; it was God who caused it to grow. All glory to God!

Be assured that God makes all things work together for the good of those who love Him. Even in the midst of pain and suffering, God is always working for our benefit, as He knows the beginning and the ending. Ephesians 2:10 states, "For we are God's handiwork, created in Christ Jesus to do good works, which God prepared in advance for us to do." God, in His divine power, sees and knows all things. His love is unfailing! I had a remarkable experience of divine intervention when my daughter-in-love, Michelle, connected me with a beautician who did my hair.

After finishing my hair, she asked if she could pray for me. I was delighted she asked if she could pray for me; I said yes. **After she prayed, she said I would finish my book this year, 2024. I asked how she knew I was writing a book. She said God said so. I was stunned at such a revelation. I began to praise and thank God for who He is- an all-knowing God who has given every believer a spiritual gift to build up His Kingdom. He demonstrated His Power clearly and vividly to me.**

God knew I needed to put my faith in Him and trust Him completely, an **Almighty God,** for I had been unconsciously denying His Power. **Still, My prayer was and is, "Lord, help me trust you more."** I rejoiced; this was so amazing- it was my first time in her presence. A couple of times, I had seen her passing in restaurants and her church. **Never had she or I had any conversation before December 31, 2023, when I sat in her chair for her to do my hair.** The name of her business is "Divine Appointment." All Praise and Glory to God!

The verse from the book of Jeremiah 29:11 in the Bible is a powerful reminder of God's love and care for us. It assures us that God has good plans for our lives and that He desires to bless us with peace, hope, and a bright future. No matter what we may be going through, we can trust that God is with us, and He is working all things together for our good. So, we can have faith and hope in Him, knowing that He will always be faithful to His promises.

God heard my earnest prayer for trusting Him more! He will rescue us. He has worked in my life in such a profound way, increasing my faith in Him through the words of someone who had no personal knowledge of me. It is a testament to the all-powerful and loving nature of our God, who is always watching over us and guiding us, even in ways we may not immediately recognize.

In March 2024, I attended our church's Jurisdictional Conference and received prayer. God revealed a health condition through the man of God of which I learned. He keeps demonstrating His miraculous power to me. The signs and wonders keep strengthening me and building my faith for the building up of His Kingdom. The Bible says, "Without faith, it is impossible to please Him." Glory to God!

The mercy and unfailing love of God is truly something to be celebrated, and I have no doubt that my faith will continue to keep me in His loving arms. A willingness to surrender ourselves completely to God is a beautiful thing. I understand the importance of dedicating my heart, soul, and mind to worshiping Him.

It is utterly amazing to think about the power and greatness of God. When we take a moment to reflect on all that He is, it is impossible not to feel grateful and in awe. One of the most comforting aspects of God is that He knows us intimately, even down to the thoughts in our hearts. He understands us better than we understand ourselves, and He is always there to guide us on the right path.

It is humbling to think that the same God who created the stars also created each and every one of us and that He has a plan for our lives that is uniquely tailored to our individual needs. When we live our lives with a healthy fear and respect for God, we can overcome the negative fears that hold us back and embrace the destiny that He has in store for us.

As we journey through life, there comes a time when we realize that we cannot do it all on our own. We need a higher power to help guide us through the challenges and uncertainties that come our way. That is where God comes in. He is the Creator who made us, and He strengthens those who are weak and tired. The Lord guides the paths of the righteous and takes pleasure in all the details of our lives. Even when we stumble and fall, He is always there to help us back up. We do not remain down.

When we put our trust in Him and let go of our worries and fears, we can experience a profound sense of peace and comfort that surpasses all understanding. Even when we don't comprehend everything that's happening, we can find solace in God's promises that His thoughts and ways are higher than ours.

May we always wholeheartedly seek the Lord and rely on His unwavering love and grace. With God beside us, we can face any challenges that come our way.

4
DELIVERANCE FROM FEAR TO VICTORY

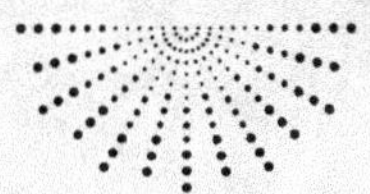

"Deliverance from fear to victory" reflects my journey of conquering my past fears and attaining success. The change from fear to victory I've experienced is my testament to God's love and grace. Fear is not a permanent state but rather a temporary obstacle that can be overcome with faith, perseverance, and determination.

By facing our fears head-on and acting towards our goals, we can transform our lives and emerge victorious. Victory is not just about achieving a particular outcome but also about the growth and transformation that occurs along the way. Glory to God!

Through all that has happened in my life, God has been demonstrating His presence and power in me and in my everyday affairs. Even in the midst of trials and tribulations, I have felt His love and mercy surrounding me like a warm blanket. And it is an amazing and joyful feeling in my heart - to know that I am not alone, that I am loved and cherished by the Creator of the universe.

Through the Holy Spirit's Power in me (*which He was all the time*), I have a peace that is sweeter than honey, a joy that cannot be taken away. Truly, it is He in me who is greater than He who is in the world. And I am forever grateful for His presence in my life.

It is a wonderful feeling to be free of the chains of fear and step into a life of victory. I am free of my fears and am now **able to share my victory with the world**. However, it takes courage and tenacity to face our fears and move past them, but **it is so worth it in the end.** It is also comforting to know that we have the Holy Spirit to guide us and help us overcome any challenges we face.

Fear used to keep me back from effectively doing God's work by staying in my comfort zone. But I refuse to be controlled by fear any longer. I am no longer afraid of what others might say, and I am no longer bound by my past. I will allow the Holy Spirit to work in me and follow God's will for His glory. "For God has not given me a spirit of fear, but of power and of love and of a sound mind."

I am so excited to share my story with you. It is incredible how fear has led me to positive changes in my life. I am able to channel fear into productive and healing ways not only for myself but also for others. For example, when I feel afraid of taking risks, I turn that fear into motivation to carefully plan and execute my actions. I also help others facing similar fears by sharing my experiences and offering support. I know that we all have the power to overcome any obstacle that weighs us down. I have empathy for those who are struggling with similar fears. I thank God for my strength and courage in these tough times.

With faith in God, we can overcome fear and walk in His peace. He has already defeated Satan. Oh, the greatness of God! All glory to God. He is the Creator of the universe and humanity, and His power is greater than any situation we face. We are more than conquerors; we gain an overwhelming victory through God's love.

God told the Apostle Paul, "My grace is sufficient for you, for My strength is made perfect in weakness" (II Corinthians 12:9). With the help of the Holy Spirit, we can continue to move forward and cast out negativity. I believe and declare that God is my refuge and strength, and I refuse to let fear have any power over me. "For God has not given us a spirit of fear, but of power and of love and of a sound mind." I know that everything is working together for my good!

I am thrilled to say that I am stronger and more resilient than ever before on my writing journey. I have stared fear in the face and emerged victorious, and I know that nothing can hold me back now. **With each passing day, I am more grateful for the challenges that have pushed me to greater heights and inspired me to step out of my comfort zone.**

God assures us through His Word that He will never leave or forsake us. We should not be afraid but trust in His promises. God's grace is His favor and goodwill that He has extended towards all of us. Through the grace of Christ, we have been provided with salvation. It is the unmerited favor that God has shown us, and He has given us everything we need to fulfill His purpose for His glory.

Prayer

Almighty God, the Creator of the universe. I give you praise; I bow in worship to honor your Name. You are worthy from the sun's rising to the going down of the same. Lord, I can face the enemy by your transforming power within me. I trust you with my life, for you love me despite my failures and weaknesses. By relying on you, God, I can do everything with you. Thank you for your everlasting love. Thank you, Lord! Have your way in our life. Amen.

5

WORSHIP, PRAISE, THANKSGIVING, AFFIRMATION

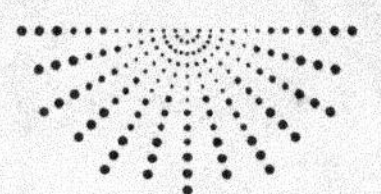

*M*editating on God's goodness fills me with deep spiritual fulfillment through worship, praise, thanksgiving, and affirmation. During these moments of reflection, I feel a profound connection to the divine and am reminded of the unending grace and love surrounding me. That memorable Tuesday night, April 7, 2020, left a lasting impact on my soul. It was a night that shook me to the core, but through it, I witnessed the wonders of God's faithfulness. Through my determination and steadfastness, I've seen His continual presence in my life, guiding me through challenges and illuminating the path ahead.

It is incredible how our unique ways of worship can lead us to a profound expression of faith. God's greatness is immeasurable, and I am constantly in awe of His goodness. Being in His presence fills me with a joy and peace that surpasses all understanding. When I think of how to worship, I am reminded of Psalms 95, 96, and 100, which reflect the awe and wonder of worship and the profound expression of faith. These Psalms celebrate the uniqueness of our worship and the incredible ways we can connect with our faith.

Also, the Psalms perfectly capture the power of our devotion to the Lord, and I am confident in my love for Him. Though the wisdom and knowledge of God are vast and beyond our comprehension, I trust in His judgments and ways. As the Psalmist beautifully says in 27:1, "The Lord is my light and my salvation; whom shall I fear?" "Oh, how deep are the riches of wisdom and knowledge of God! His judgments are unsearchable, and His ways are beyond finding out!" (Romans 11:33).

"The Creator, Maker of every perfect gift. He is our provider and the giver of life! He is King of Glory; He is Almighty, the Everlasting Father, and an All-powerful and Mighty God!" You are worthy, our Lord and God, to receive glory, honor, and power, for you created all things, and by your will they were created and have their being" (Revelation 4:11 NIV).

Praise! It is my continual "worship" of an expression of honor and gratitude to God. It is a heartfelt way to communicate with an Almighty God who hears our praise, sees our struggles, pains, and fears, and understands the constant negative thoughts that sometimes consume our minds. Expressing praise and gratitude to God can bring peace and comfort, allowing us to cope with difficulties and find hope in challenging times. By cultivating a positive attitude and trusting everything will work out, we can move forward confidently and joyfully.

Take time to appreciate the blessings in your life and express your heartfelt thanks to God. With His all-knowing presence and unbreakable source of strength, you will find comfort and guidance that cannot be found elsewhere. The Creator of heaven and earth is watching over you, and His power and love are unmatched. So, worship and praise Him with all your heart, and let His unending grace and mercy guide you through any challenge that life may bring.

It is so sweet how the power of praise can radically change our lives! As the Psalmist says, praising God is good and beautiful. It can help us shut out negative thoughts and keep the devil away from our minds. We tend to get stuck in darkness when we focus on our fears, failures, and challenges, but praise can bring light and hope to our lives.

An excellent example of the power of praise is found in the Book of Acts. Paul and Silas were beaten and imprisoned, but instead of complaining or giving up, they chose to praise God amid their pain. Their praise was so powerful that even the other prisoners heard them! And suddenly, there was a great earthquake that shook the prison's foundations and opened all the doors, setting everyone free. It is incredible what can happen when we choose to praise God despite our trials and difficulties.

With a heart full of gratitude and amazement, I lift my voice in praise to the Almighty God, who has delivered me from the shackles of fear that once held me captive. It is truly a wonder! I give thanks to God, for through His grace, I am able to overcome the negative thoughts and attacks of the enemy that seek to bring me down.

I keep rising above all my fears, failures, and obstacles, for the Lord has given me the power to do so. O Lord, our Lord, Your name is excellent all over the earth. I give You all the praise! Oh Lord, I am forever grateful for opening my eyes to see the love that You have bestowed upon me and for enabling me to work for Your good pleasure. I praise You for the gift of listening, obedience, and the ability to act with Your Power that dwells within me! I praise you, Lord!

Thanksgiving is a time to reflect on the blessings in our lives and express gratitude for them. As a believer, I acknowledge that God is the Source of all my blessings and surrender myself to His guidance and care. I am thankful for His provisions, peace, and unspeakable joy. I enter His presence with thanksgiving and make known His deeds among the people, talking of His wondrous works.

The Bible teaches us to trust in the Lord with all our hearts and to fear Him. He is the Source of all wisdom and knowledge and helps us navigate demanding situations. **It is comforting to know that we do not have to face our battles alone and that God is always with us.** Offering gratitude to our Creator is a fantastic way to show appreciation for all our blessings. As David's words of encouragement in Psalm 34:1-2, always bless the Lord and have His praise in our mouth.

It is inspiring to see how thanksgiving to God can bring joy and hope to our lives. It is also a wonderful feeling to sense the presence of the Lord deep down inside and to rejoice in His faithfulness. Hallelujah to His Name!

Affirmation, Great God Almighty, your Power is sufficient for me; your Power is made perfect in my weaknesses. I, therefore, boast the more for who you are. You know my thoughts, you know my faults, you know me better than I do myself.

Your Word says you are God, who sees every heart and understands every plan and thought. "I believe Your Word." Nothing is covered up that will not be revealed or hidden that will not be known. I am strong and courageous; you are with me and will not forsake me. I have received your Power to be a witness for you wherever I go. I am your child and have overcome the fear in my mind. More excellent are You, Lord, in me than he who is in the world.

Thank you for your divine Power to defeat the spirit of fear. Thank you for not letting me lose heart. You give your wisdom generously. So, I do not fear; you are with me. I do not have to be dismayed, for you strengthen me. You help me in all my ways. You renew my strength, to mount up with the wings like eagles, so I do not become weary and faint. You have given me your peace, so my heart is not troubled.

When I am afraid, I trust you, O Lord. I praise you; I lean on your promises and shall not be scared. Your words tell me to be strong in your strength and your mighty Power. I praise you, Lord, for your courage to stand firm in the faith. Thank you for interceding for all of us in the world. We must not be weary or discouraged because you are with us. Praise your holy Name! My trust is in you. You, God, have not given us a spirit of fear but of Power, Love, and a Sound mind. Thank you for your steadfast Love; as you guide me to be strong, I will praise your Name from whom all blessings come!

You are always with us despite what we are going through. Thank You, Lord, for your presence. You are the Lord God who takes hold of us and says do not fear; I will help you. So, I confidently speak, "The Lord is my Helper; I will not be afraid." You fight all my battles for me. Thank you, Lord. **You have empowered me with the courage to stand firm.** More than anything else, I am to guard my heart, for everything I do flows from it (Proverbs 4:23).

O God, thank you for your faith and courage. You, O Lord, are the only true and living God. Help me when I pray, believe, and do not doubt. Your Word says to cast all our cares upon you for your care. Thank you; we can give all our fears to you. You, Lord, can manage all anxieties. Amen.

6

PRAYER OF DECLARATION AND TESTIMONY

My prayer of declaration is to God the One who provides all my needs, whether I am seeking guidance, healing, or abundance.

The prayer of declaration and testimony helps me align my thoughts and words with the Almighty to connect my desires with the divine energy within and around me. A declaration prayer is a powerful way to affirm our faith and state our intentions. When we express our desires and beliefs, we reinforce them about what we want to manifest in our lives. It is a way of aligning our thoughts and words with our deepest aspirations, and it can be a transformative practice that can bring clarity, purpose, and a connection to something greater than ourselves. That is God!

I consciously surrender all things to God, the Creator who formed me, and I am thankful for His constant presence, which comforts me. I have His Spirit within me to demolish all the fiery darts of the evil one as the Spirit works in me. I am focused on who I am now as a chosen child, not on fear of the past. God empowered me to step out of my comfort zone and keep reaching. I breathe daily and feel the mighty power deep down in my soul. I am joyfully overjoyed to share my journey in pursuit of more significant achievements. I am not afraid to talk about my past mistakes now. **I can humbly tell others to look where I come from, not because I have been so good, but because of God's mercy and love.**

I appreciate the sentiment behind David's declaration of trust in the Lord as described in Psalm 23:1-6. It is a psalm that speaks to me on a personal level as well. The Lord is my shepherd, and I lack nothing in His care. Whenever I feel lost or overwhelmed, He provides me with a safe place to rest and recharge my soul. The Lord guides me along the right path, even when I face challenges or obstacles. And even in the darkest of times, I know that I have nothing to fear because He is always with me, providing comfort and protection. His blessings overflow in my life, and I know His goodness and love will follow me all the days of my life. I am so grateful to be able to dwell in the house of the Lord forever.

Although, there was a time in my life when I could not claim Psalm 23 as David proclaimed the Lord his shepherd. Today, I thank the Lord for the gift of salvation. God filled me with His Holy Spirit, giving me the power to overcome obstacles and challenges I would face. When we accept the Lord as Savior, it is through God's grace and through faith that we are saved from sin and death and empowered by the Holy Spirit to overcome any obstacle that comes our way.

I am delighted to declare that I am no longer held in bondage by fear and am able to inspire others through my testimony of what God has done in my life. **I will use my voice to spread the "Good News about God" and share with others how they can experience this life-changing power.**

My goal in these *latter years* is to tell others how God worked in my life to change me from a sinner to a Christian. I also share my story of overcoming the fear that had me bound for many years because of my past. He has given me the Power to conquer fear!

Sharing our testimonies can be incredibly powerful and impactful for us and others. Also, by sharing our experiences and how we have overcome challenges, we can provide hope and inspiration to those who may be going through similar struggles.

Sharing our testimonies can also foster community and connection, as others may relate to our experiences and feel less alone. Additionally, by sharing our testimonies, we can encourage others to share their own stories, creating a ripple effect of positivity and empowerment. Sharing our testimonies can be a beautiful way to uplift and support one another!

I heard my Pastor, Bishop Herman Crockett Jr, preach a powerful message, *"Get Excited About Jesus,"* telling his testimony and praise to what God had done for him and talking about the story of the woman at the well in John Chapter 4 where she met Jesus. The woman was so moved by this encounter that she returned to the village and told everyone, "Come see a man" who told me everything about my life.

I am overwhelmed with joy as I reflect on how God has demonstrated His power by turning my shortcomings and mistakes into something good. His grace and love have transformed my past errors into opportunities for growth and learning. I am so grateful for the way God has used my faults to shape me into a better person and guide me along the right path. Thank God for my salvation! Oh, He is an amazing God! He is the All-Powerful God. Praise you, God!

While I did not understand God's Power, His Spirit was with me from an early age. I heard in my spirit the words, ***"Greater is***

He in me than he in the world." The words reigned *in my spirit*; however, I still did not know what salvation meant, and I did the things of my human flesh. Yet, I believe my upbringing in the church impacted my life more than I understood.

God loved me while I was disobedient and still in sin. He always works things out for my good. His love for us never ceases. His Power is exceedingly great toward us who believe. Hallelujah to God!

As I matured and did fewer things of my flesh, I made a meaningful change as I surrendered my life to God. I started having the will not to do the wrong things. I desired to be pleasing to God, who saved me! Sometimes, my mind flashes back, and I think about things I was doing compared to things happening in the world today. **"I break out with a grateful heart, singing Thank you, Lord, for saving me."**

The Bible says in II Corinthians 5:17, "Therefore, if anyone is in Christ, he is a new creation; old things have passed away; behold, all things have become new." I tell the world God transformed me into a new person. I no longer desire to do the things that please my flesh. I asked God to come into my life, save me, and forgive me for my sins. I am grateful today to God for His Grace and Mercy – He saved me! He brought me out of darkness and sin.

His Word is truth! The Bible says, "For God so loved the world that He gave His one and only Son, that whoever believes in him shall not perish but have eternal life" (John 3:16). No matter your past, everyone is included in the "whoever!"

Hallelujah, "Jesus hasn't changed, for He is the same yesterday, today, and evermore." This is a powerful declaration of the timeless nature of Jesus Christ. It emphasizes the unchanging, consistent, and eternal nature of Jesus, asserting that He remains constant across all time periods. This statement is rooted in the belief that the character, love, and promises of Jesus are unwavering and enduring, providing hope and reassurance to those who follow Him. It reflects a deep sense of faith and serves as a source of comfort and strength for all believers.

The Power of God awakens the greatness of the power within us to bring good out of unpleasant situations. Nothing is too complicated for God; God can reshape and transform our lives.

"I truly believe that my experiences and insights shared in this book can serve as a source of inspiration and empowerment for those looking to overcome their obstacles and fears and pursue their dreams with confidence and resilience."

Questions to Ponder:

1. Have you faced any challenges or doubts along your spiritual journey, and if so, how did you overcome them?
2. What specific experiences or events led to your decision to surrender your life to God?
3. How has your faith impacted the way you live your life and interact with others?
4. In what ways do you seek to share your faith and the message of God's love with others?
5. Have you ever struggled with sharing your testimony? If so, how did you overcome those struggles?
6. What advice would you give to someone who wants to share their testimony but is hesitant to do so?

7

THE POWER OF PRAYER WORKS

rayer is a powerful tool that can help us find peace and strength when dealing with fear and challenging times. It is not just about speaking the right words but about having Faith and Trust in God. I have experienced the comfort and guidance that comes from prayer, which makes a real difference in our lives.

God hears our cries, sees everything, and answers our prayers even when the answer is "wait" or "no." The Power of prayer is truly remarkable. It has the ability to bring healing to any problem, whether it be fear or any other obstacle. When we turn to God, He shows up to guide us with His infinite wisdom and strength. He is the "Great I am God," and everything we need can be found in His Power.

Through prayer, we can cultivate qualities of the fruit of the Spirit, such as love, joy, peace, patience, kindness, goodness, faithfulness, gentleness, and self-control. By seeking God's presence and aligning our hearts with His will through prayer, we can experience a transformation that manifests these virtues in our lives. This fruit blooms within us, and our outward actions and attitudes become a reflection of God's grace; therefore, we can live a life that is pleasing to Him. Let us join together to seek God's guidance and allow His grace to shine through us.

The power of prayer is truly transformative and has the potential to impact our lives in ways beyond our imagination. Both prayer and faith hold vital positions in our lives. The teachings of the Bible emphasize the significance of believing in God and His plan for our lives. Through prayer, we can connect with God and seek His guidance and support.

Prayer provides a source of hope and peace in a world that can feel chaotic and unpredictable. Although life may present challenges, we are encouraged to focus on God and offer Him gratitude and praise daily. By doing so, we can develop resilience and perseverance and experience the salvation of the Lord. Through Jesus Christ, we can overcome any obstacle and find peace amid any storm.

Wow, it is incredible how God can protect us in need. I remember when Hurricane Isabel hit in 2003 and how all the trees around my neighbor's houses were knocked down, but miraculously, none fell on my property. I knew it was only through God's protection that I was spared. I know that God will protect us when we call upon Him.

Throughout Bible History, it assures us we can trust in God's Word. A splendid example is in 2 Chronicles 20 of the Bible; there is a story about a King who cried out to God when a great multitude was coming against him and his people. He said, "For we have no power against this great multitude that is coming against us; nor do we know what to do, but our **eyes are upon You.**" God sent His Word, "Do not be afraid or discouraged—for the battle is not yours, but God's.

Whether our battles are large or small, God can and will fight them. Set our eyes upon Him, trust Him, and have Faith in Him. God can provide for us in unusual ways. For instance, when I struggled to pass an accounting class, God placed me under a patient and compassionate teacher who helped me understand the material better. I know His divine Power can provide everything we need, and I trust Him to do so.

It is reassuring to know that we are never truly alone and that there is always God's help to turn to when we need help.

Whenever I am feeling down or facing challenges, my God, I call upon, and He always answers. Through prayer and faith, we can surrender our fears; He provides protection, comfort, guidance, and support. Prayer has been a reliable source of comfort and encouragement to me.

He engages in every aspect of my life, from my daily routine to my finances and clothing choices. Although I may sometimes falter, I am grateful for my faith in God as I approach my twilight years, during which I have grown stronger. I trust and know that God has my best interests at heart and will always guide me toward making wise choices.

Jesus's love is a constant source of strength and comfort for those who follow Him. His unwavering and enduring promises bring hope and reassurance, reminding us that we are never alone in our journey. As we navigate life's challenges, we can find solace in His love and take comfort in His unfailing promises, knowing that He is always by our side.

I praise God for His faithfulness, goodness, and unending love. The peace and joy I experience in His presence are unparalleled, and I am grateful for His constant support. I am experiencing a deep sense of joy as I write about my experience of God's incredible transformative Power. I give God all the thanks and glory for His boundless Power; He can do exceedingly above all I can ask or think. Beyond any doubt, I know God's Power is a healer for everything. I am so grateful for God's great move in my life.

I emphasize! Prayer will keep us connected to God and help us overcome our fears and worries. Prayer keeps me abiding in Him and He in me, and I surrender everything to Him. There is no problem God cannot heal, whether it be fear or other things. God will show up to guide us. He is the "Great I am God." Everything we need is in His power! The power of prayer works! It grows beautiful fruit in me! My salvation has bloomed through prayer into an outward manifestation of God's grace!

Prayer gives me the power, spiritual discernment, and wisdom to do the right things. I read in the Bible that God will keep one's mind at peace because of trust in Him. He cares about all our needs. His Word tells us to cast everything upon Him. I give Him Praise! Through prayer, I gained the courage, strength, and confidence to use my gift of public speaking on Facebook. I am telling of God's tremendous Power through social media.

Prayer is the great privilege God has given us access to him. It is the foundation of hope, love, joy, and peace. Despite the things of the flesh, God is the healer. I rejoice to talk and listen for guidance from the All-Knowing God. It is so sweet to pour my heart out before the Lord, drawing nearer to Him through prayer. **My earnest and sincere desire is to please God.**

Paul's prayer for spiritual empowerment is a beautiful and excellent example for us to follow. It is lovely to see how he prayed for not just his spiritual growth but also for others. We can all benefit from praying for inner strength, understanding God's love, and being filled with the fullness of God. It is a beautiful reminder of the Power of prayer and how it can transform our lives and the lives of those around us (Ephesians verses 1:15-21).

We are also reminded to be strong in the Lord and the Power of His might and to put on the whole armor of God so that we can stand against the schemes of the devil. It means girding our waist with the truth of God's Word and putting on the breastplate of righteousness.

Moreover, we are encouraged to take up the shield of Faith, which can extinguish all the flaming arrows of the evil one, and to put on the helmet of salvation and the sword of the Spirit, which is the Word of God. Additionally, we are urged to pray in the Spirit on all occasions with all kinds of prayers and requests and to be alert at all times, praying for all the Lord's people (Ephesians 6:10-18). The words of the Apostle Paul to the Ephesians are very encouraging and instructive.

It is awe-inspiring how the Power of Faith and Hope can push us beyond our limits and help us overcome our fears and challenges. The strength and resilience we need to face life's most challenging moments come from within us, and it is up to us to embrace it with courage and determination. As the Bible says, those who trust the Lord will renew their strength and soar like eagles (Isaiah 40:31). It is a beautiful message of hope and encouragement that we can all hold onto in times of hardship.

We must always be prayerful and watchful that the devil, like a roaring lion, is constantly seeking to devour us. Therefore, it is essential to remain alert and of sober mind so that we can recognize and resist his tactics. By submitting our thoughts to God, we can experience the perfect peace from His protection and strength. Remember, we have been given power through Christ to overcome the enemy, whether fear or other challenges.

Jesus taught us to abide in Him to bear fruit because we cannot succeed apart from Him. Stay connected to God, for He is our Source and our strength. Do not allow fear to hinder your potential. Have faith in God and persist in pursuing your goals.

"The Word of God is indeed alive and powerful. When Jesus was tempted by the devil in the wilderness, He used the Word to overcome Satan's attacks. The Word of God is said to be sharper than any double-edged sword, and it can even divide soul and spirit, joints and marrow, and judge the thoughts and attitudes of the heart" (Hebrews 4:12).

I'm grateful to God for giving me the strength to persevere through tough times, overcome challenges, and conquer my fears. All glory to God! With the help of the Holy Spirit, I am empowered to overcome. As the chosen ones, we are called to be the light of the world and have power over the enemy in every aspect of our lives. I declare that Jesus is Lord over fear in every area of my life, and I surrender to Him completely.

As believers, we find comfort and guidance in the Word of God. The Bible teaches us that when we encounter difficulties and challenges in life, we should embrace them with a joyful heart because we know that these trials will test our faith and strengthen our perseverance. By persevering through these trials, we can grow and mature as individuals, becoming more complete and lacking nothing (James 1:2-4).

Prayer

Almighty God, Lord of heaven and earth, thank you for keeping me through my teenage years into adulthood. I am so grateful to you for keeping me through all the mistakes I made in my life. You still love me! Thank you for longsuffering with me in my inactions of letting the hostile spirit of fear be a stronghold in my life. Indeed, your Word is the balm for all of my healings. I am healed mentally, physically, spiritually, socially, and in every way.

Your Word says; therefore, I tell you, whatever things you ask when you pray, believe that you receive them, and *I* will have them. Thank you for all your promises. Thank you for making a way for every area of my life. Above all things, you *wish I may* prosper and be healthy, even as *my* soul prospers. Thank You, Lord, for breaking the stronghold of fear in my life! You are so gracious and merciful. Hallelujah to your Name! I give You the Praise! Amen.

Questions To Ponder:

1. In what ways have you seen prayer positively impact your life and the lives of those around you?
2. How has your faith in God helped you overcome challenges in your life?
3. How do you think sharing personal stories can inspire and uplift others?
4. What advice would you give to someone who is struggling to find joy and peace in their life?
5. Can you share any particular moments or experiences where you felt God's presence in your life?

8

EQUIPPED WITH POWER, LOVE, AND A SOUND MIND

As you reach the final pages of this book, I hope you carry with you the realization that you are equipped with power, fueled by love, and blessed with a sound mind. Embrace these gifts as you journey through life, and may they guide you toward fulfilling your dreams and inspiring others. Remember that you have the strength within you to overcome any challenge, the love to light your way, and the clarity of mind to make profound, positive choices. May this book serve as a testament to the incredible potential that resides within you.

Keep shining bright and impacting the world with your unique gifts and abilities. Equipped with power, love, and a sound mind, you and I can make wise decisions. This power enables us to have foresight and use discretion, serving as a guide for personal growth, inspiration, and love. It is a beautiful combination that empowers you and me to live a fulfilling life.

This power helps us in ways that surpass human understanding while working on our excellent purpose and destiny. It nurtures our spiritual selves and provides us with the abilities, talents, and skills we need for this life. I am now more confident in declaring that I am more tuned into my spiritual self and am endowed with power, love, and a sound mind.

With a renewed mind, I deliberately respond wholeheartedly with courage, boldness, and confidence, for I have been given the power. Negative thinking and self-doubt cannot limit or hinder me anymore.

Recognizing the presence of the Holy Spirit in my life has allowed me to tap into my inner strength and wisdom to overcome obstacles and find balance. It's important to understand that acknowledging the guidance of the Holy Spirit does not mean that I am perfect or superhuman. Despite my best efforts and intentions, I sometimes falter, but these situations serve as opportunities for growth and learning rather than failures. I welcome the journey of self-improvement, knowing that facing challenges along the way is normal.

Thus, I engage in positive self-talk, continuously pursue personal development, and refuse to succumb to setbacks. With my faith in God, I firmly believe in my ability to persist and surmount challenges. Drawing resilience from within, I can bounce back, forgive, and set myself free. I am resolute in my determination to persevere until I reach my objectives. I rely on my faith and inner strength to navigate difficult times and maintain a composed and clear mindset, even in the face of adversity. This inner strength enables me to cultivate profound self-awareness and foster self-love.

The inner strength I've developed has allowed me to deepen my self-awareness and nurture self-love. It has made me more attuned to my inner power, giving me a deeper understanding of what it means to experience inner peace and contentment. This newfound clarity has enriched my life in numerous ways, helping me to navigate challenges with greater confidence and composure.

Writing these eight chapters has been a liberating experience. Waking up early to write has also helped me tap into my inner peace and power. It has allowed me to express gratitude, joy, and the beauty and peace surrounding me. Through this process, I have engaged in self-reflection and introspection, addressing the fear from my past. It has brought newfound clarity into my life, enriching it in numerous ways and helping me to face challenges with greater confidence and composure.

Additionally, my age, maturity, faith, and belief in God have played a vital role.

In addition, I have found that listening to spiritual and instrumental music, tuning into the quiet voice within my soul, praying and fasting, as well as refraining from watching television, have all played a significant role in my life.

I aimed to deepen my understanding of my personal values and beliefs while nurturing my spiritual growth. I have reached a level of maturity and am committed to living a life of integrity and honor, always staying true to my Word. In the quiet of solitude, I discovered the patience and discipline needed to uphold my beliefs and values, and I dedicated myself to treating others with the same respect and kindness that I would wish to receive.

The shift in my mindset has given me the power to pursue my goals and aspirations with determination and resilience. I now face challenges with a positive and confident mindset, enabling me to confront obstacles without being hindered by my thoughts and fears.

Seeking wisdom and surrendering everything while relying on the power of God can help us overcome negative fears and other life challenges. Believing that we can do everything through Christ, who strengthens us, is essential. **The Word of God assures us that we have not been given a spirit of fear but rather one of power, love, and a sound mind. Only an all-powerful, holy God can provide us with everything we need to live without fear. The power to overcome resides within us, waiting to be activated and manifested.**

Power of Love! The power of love is truly remarkable. It can unite people, heal old wounds, and inspire great acts of kindness. Love has the power to uplift us during our lowest moments and give us strength to overcome obstacles. It motivates us to be better versions of ourselves and encourages empathy, compassion, and mutual understanding. The power of love knows no bounds and can change the world for the better.

Love is a powerful characteristic that God has given us. It can inspire us to be strong, brave, and purposeful. It is important to show kindness to others, even when they do not show it back. Love comes from God and is demonstrated through His unfailing love for us. The Bible teaches us that we should love each other as Jesus loved us, which is the most excellent form of love.

"Love is patient, kind, and humble. It does not envy, boast, or dishonor others. Instead, it seeks to forgive and is not easily angered. We should love God with all our hearts, souls, and minds and love our neighbors as ourselves." Love has the power to cover many sins, and we should always strive to show it in our daily lives. Believe in yourself and trust in God's plan for you. The tremendous power of God can transform us from the inside out.

Along with the characteristics of love, according to the Bible, **a sound mind** is characterized by self-control, discipline, and good judgment. Knowing that God empowers us with power, love, and a sound mind is reassuring. The Holy Spirit is within us to guide us in making good decisions, bless our minds, and help us grow in God's things. King Solomon is an excellent example of someone who sought wisdom from God to lead His people. God was pleased with Solomon's request and gave him understanding.

We, too, can ask God for wisdom and guidance. Jesus' words about abiding in Him are powerful and reassuring. When we abide in Him, we are connected to the Source of all wisdom and understanding. It is a beautiful feeling that we have been created in God's image and can choose to abide in Him. Nothing is hidden from God, and in Him, we can find the answer to everything we go through. All praise and glory to God, our Creator, who loves and cares for us.

A sound mind is essential for leading a fulfilling life. It allows us to think, make better decisions, and maintain healthy relationships. When our mind is at peace, we are better equipped to manage life's challenges and enjoy its joys. It is truly liberating to have control over our thoughts and emotions. We must be mindful of what we allow into our minds and focus on things that bring us joy, excitement, and encouragement. I am glad to share that God has given me the strength to walk free of fear and that I can share His blessings with others.

I am empowered to expand myself in love to a hurting world, guided by the infinite power of God. This soundness of mind allows me to enjoy the beautiful energy of peace and love that resides within me and radiates to others. It is the tremendous power of the Creator's light shining and is shining through me.

The soundness of my mind moves me to pray for others who are going through trials and troubles. As I operate with the wellness of mind, I receive my blessing while being a blessing to others. Praying and showing love and kindness to others is what I am to do, no matter what race or creed. He has shown His Love to us by dying on the cross. The love of God in my heart helps me to effectively use God's Word against the enemy's attacks, enabling me to take authority over the thoughts that come to my mind. A sound sense of wisdom that keeps driving me to be faithful for my freedom to victory has already been won.

I am exceedingly excited to have the power of a sound mind to overcome challenges, especially the challenges of fear I have been writing about. I know that I am not alone in my struggles. It is fascinating how fear has catalyzed positive change and personal growth in my life. This emotion has stirred me up and pushed me to take actions I might never have considered. As I stated earlier, when we face our fears and confront them head-on, we open ourselves up to new possibilities and experiences that can work for our good. I thank the Lord; He gave me the power to harness the power of fear to make a meaningful change in my life, as I have repeatedly said throughout my writing.

"Our experiences play a significant role in shaping our lives. They can take us on unexpected paths that we never thought we would travel."

Embracing the journey and learning from our experiences can be a powerful catalyst for personal growth and development. With a renewed mind, you have the opportunity to approach life with a cheerful outlook and make the most out of every situation. It's important to embrace the journey and learn from our experiences. It can be a powerful realization. It is amazing how our experiences shape us and can lead us down unexpected paths.

"Have you ever heard the saying feel the fear and do it anyway?" It is a powerful reminder that fear does not have to hold us back from achieving our goals. Sometimes, taking that first step toward something new can be scary, but it is important to remember that growth often comes from stepping out of our comfort zones. So, the next time you are feeling afraid, try to push through it and act towards your dreams.

POWER TO CONQUER FEAR!

"You might be surprised at what you can accomplish!"

ABOUT THE AUTHOR

Doretha Smith
Retiree
United States Postal Service

Dear reader, thank you for purchasing this book. I thank God, for He has given us tremendous power through His Holy Spirit. With this power comes the ability to do wonderful things, to love deeply, and to have a sound mind. Imagine our impact on the world if we all harnessed this power! I am grateful for the opportunity to author this book, and I pray that the Holy Spirit will breathe afresh in all who read it. May its message inspire and guide you, and may you experience the love of God in ever-increasing measure. May we all join together and thank Almighty God for His abundant blessings! We can make a positive difference with His Holy Spirit as our guide.

It has been a joy to author this book and tell of your Power, God. This book could never have been without you, God giving me the courage, boldness, and perseverance not to let **fear** continue to keep me in captivity.

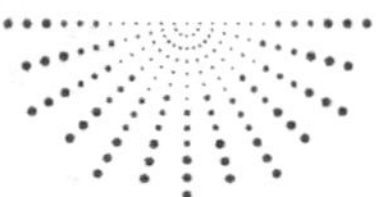

Doretha Smith is a member of Faith and Hope Temple COGIC, Petersburg, VA 23803-3635.

Doretha loves praying and encouraging others. She has been leading the intercessory prayer ministry for over twenty years at her church.

Her mission is to be a yielded vessel to the work of building God's Kingdom, interceding, and ministering to hurting souls.

I can be contacted.
Email: smithd01@aol.com

9 798893 838596